Sunday 7,

Carol-Ann McKenna.

174 Collinswood, Dublin. → 6:30.

DCU. opposite   inside church.

Monday 8pm.

prompt.recordings@btinternet.com   us.
ulla@500x.net.

The Heavenly Christmas Tree

Priest.
Jesu Joy.
Vivaldi.

Release 1 + 6.7   6th Nov

Second + last are hardest.

20 August

The Heavenly Christmas Tree

A Cantata for
Youth Choir   Adult Choir
Soloists   Audience   Reader
Flute   Percussion   Piano

Colin Mawby

Kevin Mayhew

We hope you enjoy *The Heavenly Christmas Tree*.
Further copies are available from your local music shop or Christian bookshop.

In case of difficulty, please contact the publisher direct:

The Sales Department
KEVIN MAYHEW LTD
Rattlesden
Bury St Edmunds
Suffolk IP30 0SZ

Phone 0449 737978
Fax 0449 737834

Please ask for our complete catalogue of outstanding Church Music.

Front Cover: *Detail of Heaven from the Last Judgement* by Fra Angelico (c.1387-1485).
Reproduced by courtesy of Museo di san Marco Dell'Angelico, Florence/
Bridgeman Art Library, London.

Cover design: Juliette Clarke and Graham Johnstone.
Picture Research: Jane Rayson.

First published in Great Britain in 1993 by Kevin Mayhew Ltd.

ISBN 0 86209 418 6

Printed and bound in Great Britain.

Contents

This work is scored for the following:

Youth Choir
Adult Choir
Two Soprano Soloists from the Adult Choir
Soprano and Alto Soloists*
Soprano Solo (off-stage)** from the Youth Choir
Soloists from the Youth Choir
Audience
Reader
Flute
Percussion (2 players)
Piano

* These two soloists may be taken from the Adult Choir.

** The off-stage soloist should be positioned in a high gallery and may be amplified. If necessary this part may be taken by an adult.

For Beverley, Benedict and Clement

THE HEAVENLY CHRISTMAS TREE

Colin Mawby (b.1936)

FIRST MOVEMENT
Glory's Dawn

Youth Choir: When our Lord's lov-ing mind, thought to save lost man-kind, on-ly one could he find

Adult Choir: When our Lord's lov-ing mind, thought to save lost man-kind, on-ly one could he find

Youth Choir: pure and free of sin - ning, grace and fa - vour win - ning. O the night is day:

Adult Choir: pure and free of sin - ning, grace and fa - vour win - ning. O the night is day:

Audience: O the night is day:

9

* This carol opens and closes the cantata. The percussion should only play during the Cantata's conclusion.

14

15

Second Movement
I sing of a maiden that is makéless
All my heart this night rejoices
Lullay my liking

16

17

19

25

27

30

31

38

40

saw a fair mai - den   sit - ten and sing: she   lul - lèd a lit - tle child,   a swee - te lord-ing.   Lul-lay my lik - ing,

saw a fair mai - den   sit - ten and sing: she   lul - lèd a lit - tle child,   a swee - te lord-ing.   Lul-lay my lik - ing,

Ah

Ah   Ah

Ah

Ah

* The bottom C♯ is optional.

42

44

45

49

THIRD MOVEMENT
The Carnal and the Crane

✶ indicates a hand-clap.

'Li' should be sung as in 'little'. It should be sung very lightly.

* All humming should be performed with slightly opened lips.

61

64

FOURTH MOVEMENT
O my deir hert

69

THE HEAVENLY CHRISTMAS TREE

The Heavenly Christmas Tree

Fedor Mikhailovich Dostoevsky

I AM A NOVELIST, and I suppose I have made up this story. I write 'I suppose', though I know for a fact that I have made it up, but yet I keep fancying that it must have happened somewhere at some time, that it must have happened on Christmas Eve in some great town in a time of terrible frost.

I have a vision of a boy, a little boy, six years old or even younger. This boy woke up that morning in a cold damp cellar. He was dressed in a sort of little dressing-gown and was shivering with cold. There was a cloud of white steam from his breath, and sitting on a box in the corner, he blew the steam out of his mouth and amused himself in his dullness watching it float away. But he was terribly hungry. Several times that morning he went up to the plank bed where his sick mother was lying on a mattress as thin as a pancake, with some sort of bundle under her head for a pillow. How had she come here? She must have come with her boy from some other town and suddenly fallen ill. The landlady who let the 'corners' had been taken two days before to the police station, the lodgers were out and about as the holiday was so near, and the only one left had been lying for the last twenty-four hours dead drunk, not having waited for Christmas. In another corner of the room a wretched old woman of eighty, who had once been a children's nurse but was now left to die friendless, was moaning and groaning with rheumatism, scolding and grumbling at the boy so that he was afraid to go near her corner. He had got a drink of water in the outer room, but could not find a crust anywhere, and had been on the point of waking his mother a dozen times. He felt frightened at last in the darkness: it had long been dusk, but no light was kindled. Touching his mother's face, he was surprised that she did not move at all, and that she was as cold as the wall. 'It is very cold here,' he thought. He stood a little, unconsciously letting his hands rest on the dead woman's shoulders, then he breathed on his fingers to warm them, and then quietly fumbling for his cap on the bed, he went out of the cellar. He would have gone earlier, but was afraid of the big dog which had been howling all day at the neighbour's door at the top of the stairs. But the dog was not there now, and he went out into the street.

Mercy on us, what a town! He had never seen anything like it before. In the town from which he had come, it was always such black darkness at night. There was one lamp for the whole street, the little, low-pitched, wooden houses were closed up with shutters, there was no one to be seen in the street after dusk, all the people shut themselves up in their houses, and there was nothing but the howling of packs of dogs, hundreds and thousands of them barking and howling all night. But there it was so warm and he was given food, while here – oh dear, if he only had something to eat! And what a noise and rattle here, what light and what people, horses and carriages, and what a frost! The frozen steam hung in clouds over the horses, over their warmly breathing mouths; their hoofs clanged against the stones through the powdery snow, and everyone pushed so, and – oh, dear, how he longed for some morsel to eat, and how wretched he suddenly felt. A policeman walked by and turned away to avoid seeing the boy.

Here was another street – oh, what a wide one, here he would be run over for certain; how everyone was shouting, racing and driving along, and the light, the light! And what was this? A huge glass window, and through the window a tree reaching up to the ceiling; it was a fir tree, and on it were ever so many lights, gold papers and apples and little dolls and horses; and there were children clean and dressed in their best running about the room, laughing and playing and eating and drinking something. And then a little girl began dancing with one of the boys, what a pretty little girl! And he could hear the music through the window. The boy looked and wondered and laughed, though his toes were aching with the cold and his fingers were red and stiff so that it hurt him to move them. And all at once the boy remembered how his toes and fingers hurt him, and began crying, and ran on; and again through another window-pane he saw another Christmas tree, and on a table cakes of all sorts – almond cakes, red cakes and yellow cakes, and three grand young ladies were sitting there, and they gave the cakes to anyone who went up to them, and the door kept opening, lots of gentlemen and ladies went in from the street. The boy crept up, suddenly opened the door and went in. Oh, how they shouted at him and waved him back! One lady went up to him hurriedly and slipped a kopeck into his hand, and with her own hands opened the door into the street for him ! How frightened he was. And the kopeck rolled away and clinked upon the steps; he could not bend his red fingers to hold it tight. The boy ran away and went on, where he did not know. He was ready to cry again but he was afraid, and ran on and on and blew his fingers. And he was miserable because he felt suddenly so lonely and terrified, and all at once, mercy on us! What was this again? People were standing in a crowd admiring. Behind a glass window there were three little dolls, dressed in red and green dresses, and exactly, exactly as though they were alive. One was a little old man sitting and playing a big violin, the two others were standing close by and playing little violins and nodding in time, and looking at one another, and their lips moved, they were speaking, actually speaking, only one couldn't hear through the glass. And at first the boy thought they were alive, and when he grasped that they were dolls he laughed. He had never seen such dolls before, and had no idea there were such dolls! And he wanted to cry, but he felt amused, amused by the dolls. All at once he fancied that someone caught at his smock behind: a wicked big boy was standing beside him and suddenly hit him on the head, snatched off his cap and tripped him up. The boy fell down on the ground, at once there was a shout, he was numb with fright, he jumped up and ran away. He ran and, not knowing where he was going, ran in at the gate of someone's courtyard, and sat down behind a stack of wood: 'They won't find me here, besides it's dark!'

He sat huddled up and was breathless from fright, and all at once, quite suddenly, he felt so happy: his hands and feet suddenly left off aching and grew so warm, as warm as though he were on a stove; then he shivered all over, then he gave a start, why, he must have been asleep. How nice to have a sleep here! 'I'll sit here a little and go and look at the dolls again,' said the boy, and smiled thinking of them. 'Just as though they were alive! . . .' And suddenly he heard his mother singing over him. 'Mammy, I am asleep; how nice it is to sleep here!'

'Come to my Christmas tree, little one,' a soft voice suddenly whispered over his head.

He thought that this was still his mother, but no, it was not she. Who it was calling him, he could not see, but someone bent over and embraced him in the darkness; and he stretched out his hands to him, and . . . and all at once – oh, what a bright light! Oh, what a Christmas tree! And yet it was not a fir tree, he had never seen a tree like that! Where was he now? Everything was bright and shining, and all round him were dolls; but no, they were not dolls, they were little boys and girls, only so bright and shining. They all came flying round him, they all kissed him, took him and carried him along with them, and he was flying himself, and he saw that his mother was looking at him and laughing joyfully. 'Mammy, Mammy; oh, how nice it is here, Mammy!' And again he kissed the children and wanted to tell them at once of those dolls in the shop window. 'Who are you, boys? Who are you, girls?' he asked, laughing and admiring them.

'This is Christ's Christmas tree,' they answered. 'Christ always has a Christmas tree on this day, for the little children who have no tree of their own . . .' And he found out that all these little boys and girls were children just like himself; that some had been frozen in the baskets in which they had as babies been laid on the doorsteps of well-to-do Petersburg people, others had been boarded out with Finnish women by the Foundling and had been suffocated, others had died at their starved mother's breasts (in the Samara famine), others had died in the third-class railway carriages from the foul air; and yet they were all here, they were all like angels about Christ, and He was in the midst of them and held out His hands to them and blessed them and their mothers . . . And the mothers of these children stood on one side weeping; each one knew her boy or girl, and the children flew up to them and kissed them and wiped away their tears with their little hands, and begged them not to weep because they were so happy.

And down below in the morning the porter found the little dead body of the frozen child on the woodstack; they sought out his mother too . . . She had died before him. They met before the Lord God in heaven.

Why have I made up such a story, so out of keeping with an ordinary diary, and a writer's above all? And I promised two stories dealing with real events! But that is just it, I keep fancying that all this may have happened really – that is, what took place in the cellar and on the woodstack; but as for Christ's Christmas tree, I cannot tell you whether that could have happened or not.

SIXTH MOVEMENT
The Oxen

Christ·mas Eve and twelve of the clock: 'Now they are all on their

Ah

Ah

Perc.

S Solo

knees,' an el-der said, as we sat in a flock by the em-bers in hearth-side

Youth Choir

S

Ah

A

Ah

Perc.

S Solo

ease.

Youth Choir

S

We pic-tured the meek mild crea-tures where they dwelt in their straw-y

A

We pic-tured the meek mild crea-tures where they dwelt in their straw-y

75

78

SEVENTH MOVEMENT
All and Some
Ben Johnson's Carol
The Gospel of John 1:1,4,5,14

No-well sing we, both

all and some, now Rex pa-ci-fi-cus is y-come, ex-or-tum est in love and

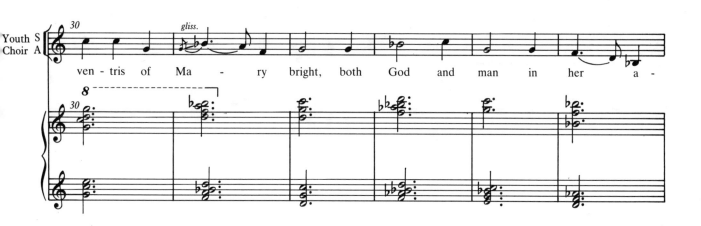

* Sing this passage with a nasal quality.

85

* The bottom C is optional.

94

97

99

103

Repeat First Movement

107

Textual Sources

Glory's Dawn
Mark Woodruff (b. 1959)

I sing of a maiden
Medieval English Carol

All my heart this night rejoices
Paulus Gerhardt (1606-1676)
translated by Catherine Winkworth (1827-1878)

Lullay my liking
The Sloane MS (c.15th century)

The Carnal and the Crane
Traditional Medieval Carol

O my deir hert, young Jesus sweit
Anonymous

The Heavenly Christmas Tree
Fedor Mikhailovich Dostoevsky (1821-1881)
translated by Constance Garnett
Text reproduced by kind permission of William Heinemann Limited.

The Oxen
Thomas Hardy (1840-1928)

All and Some
Seldon MS (c.1450)

Ben Johnson's Carol
Ben Johnson (1573-1637)

The Gospel of John 1:1,4,5,14
Authorised Version